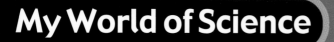

My World of Science

USING ELECTRICITY

Angela Royston

Heinemann
LIBRARY

www.heinemann.co.uk/library
Visit our website to find out more information about **Heinemann Library** books.

To order:
☎ Phone 44 (0) 1865 888066
▤ Send a fax to 44 (0) 1865 314091
▯ Visit the Heinemann Bookshop at www.heinemann.co.uk/library to browse our catalogue and order online.

First published in Great Britain by Heinemann Library, Halley Court, Jordan Hill, Oxford, OX2 8EJ, a division of Reed Educational & Professional Publishing Ltd. Heinemann is a registered trademark of Reed Educational & Professional Publishing Ltd.

OXFORD   MELBOURNE   AUCKLAND   JOHANNESBURG   BLANTYRE
GABORONE   IBADAN   PORTSMOUTH NH (USA)   CHICAGO

Designed by bigtop, Bicester, UK
Originated by Ambassador Litho Ltd.
Printed and bound in Hong Kong/China

06 05 04 03 02
10 9 8 7 6 5 4 3 2

06 05 04 03 02
10 9 8 7 6 5 4 3 2 1

ISBN 0 431 13716 1 (hardback)

ISBN 0 431 13722 6 (paperback)

British Library Cataloguing in Publication Data
Royston, Angela
Using electricity. – (My world of science)
1. Electricity – Juvenile literature
I. Title
537

Acknowledgements
The Publishers would like to thank the following for permission to reproduce photographs:
Corbis: pp5, 8, 25; Trevor Clifford: pp6, 7, 9, 10, 11, 12, 13, 14, 15, 16, 17, 18, 19, 20, 21, 22, 23, 24, 26, 27, 28, 29; Trip: H Rogers p4.

Cover photograph reproduced with permission of Corbis.

Every effort has been made to contact copyright holders of any material reproduced in this book. Any omissions will be rectified in subsequent printings if notice is given to the Publisher.

KNOWSLEY LIBRARY SERVICE

Please return this book on or before the date shown below

PROJECT LOAN

You may return this book to any Knowsley library
For renewal please telephone
Halewood - 486 4442   Housebound Service - 443 4223
Huyton/Mobile - 443 3734/5   Kirkby - 443 4290/89
Page Moss - 489 9814   Prescot - 426 6449
School Library Service - 443 4202
Stockbridge Village - 480 3925   Whiston - 426 4757
http://www.knowsley.gov.uk/

Contents

Any words appearing in the text in bold, **like this**, are explained in the Glossary.

What is electricity?

Electricity is a **power** or **force** that can make something work. For example, electricity makes this bulb light up.

Electricity is used in **machines** in schools, shops, offices and even in the street. The signs above use electricity to light them.

Using electricity

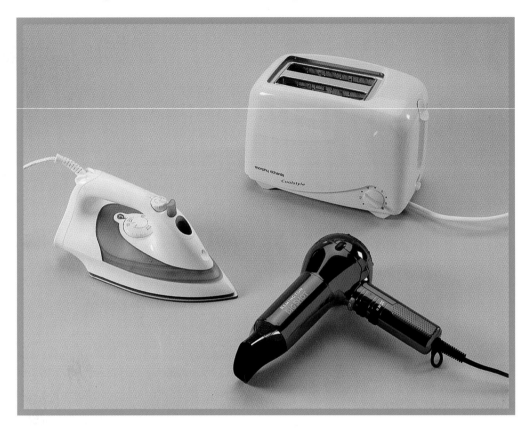

Electrical **power** can be changed into heat, noise or movement as well as into light. These **machines** all use electricity to make heat.

A television uses electricity to make pictures and sounds. A vacuum cleaner uses electricity to suck up dust. It also makes a lot of noise!

Where does electricity come from?

Electricity is made in **power stations**. It is sent along wires to houses, shops and other buildings. The electrical wires are joined to **sockets** in the wall.

When an electric plug is pushed into a socket, electricity flows into the **machine**. Some sockets have **switches** that stop the electricity flowing.

Danger!

Be careful – electricity is dangerous.
An electric shock may hurt or kill you.
Never poke things into **sockets** or
electrical **machines**.

Once an electric iron, toaster or oven is hot, it can take a long time to cool down. Be careful not to touch these things after they have been used.

What is a battery?

A battery is a store of electricity.
Chemicals inside the battery slowly
change to make electricity. Batteries
are made in different shapes and sizes.

Batteries make only a small amount of electricity and so are very safe. How many batteries does this **remote control** need to make it work?

Machines that use batteries

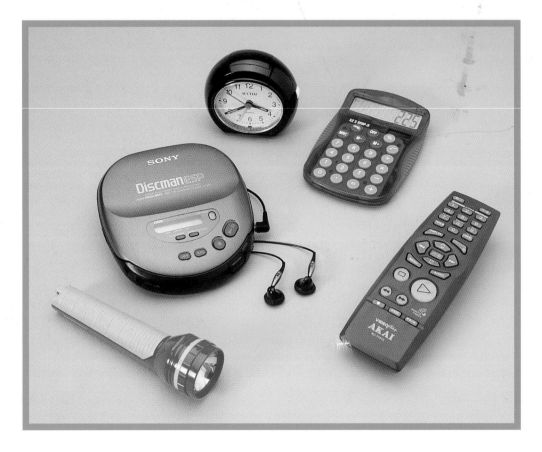

Batteries are useful because you can carry them around. All of these **machines** use batteries so that you can take them around with you.

Batteries do not last for ever. After a while they cannot make electricity. When the batteries in these toys are used up, the toys will stop working.

Taking a torch apart

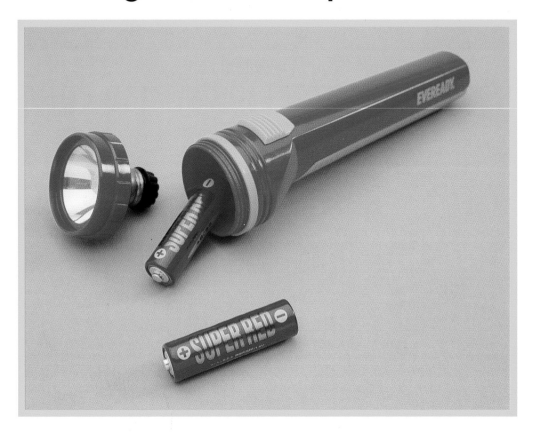

Look at one of the batteries inside a torch. One end is flat and has a − sign on the side. The other end has a bump with a + sign.

Each battery has to be the right way round to make the torch work. The + end of the battery touches the + sign in the torch.

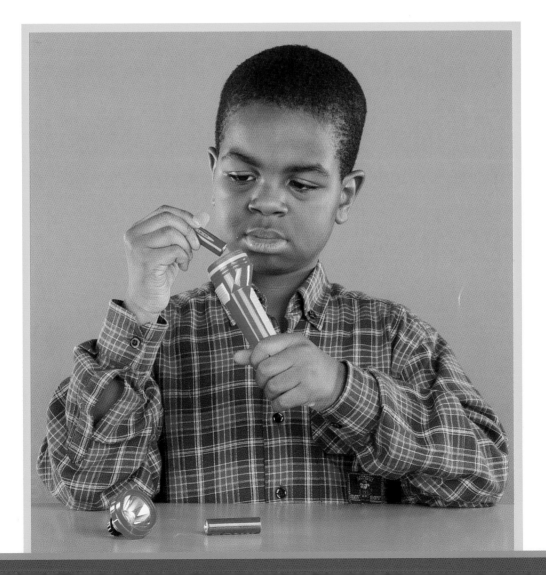

What is a circuit?

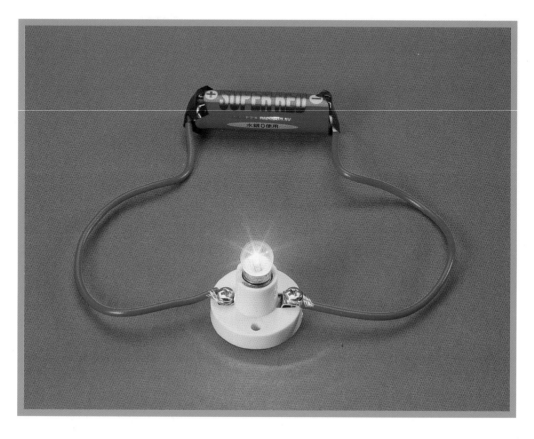

A **circuit** is a pathway for electricity to flow along. Electricity flows from the battery through the wire, through the light bulb and back to the battery.

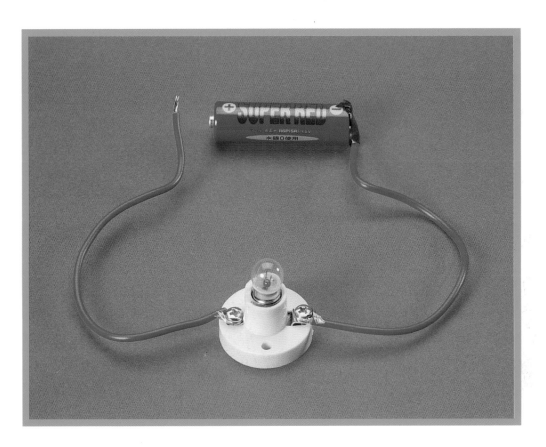

Electricity will flow only if the pathway
makes a complete loop. Here the loop
has been broken. The electricity stops
flowing and the light goes out.

Lighting two bulbs

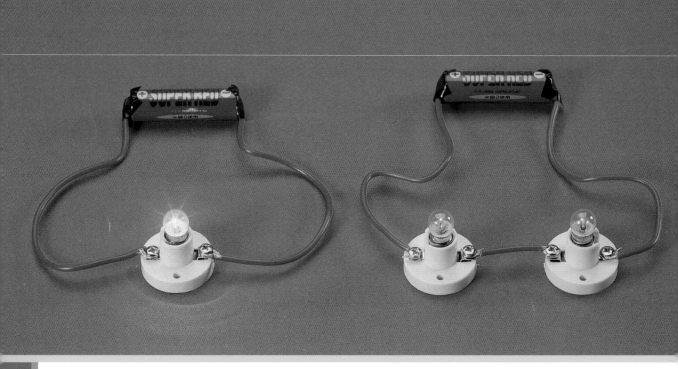

You can add one or more bulbs to a **circuit**. But every time you add one, the light from each bulb will be dimmer.

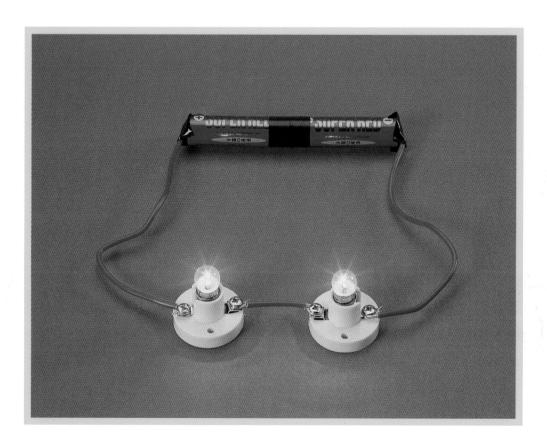

A battery can only make a fixed amount of electricity. If you add another battery, it adds more electricity. Now the bulbs shine brighter.

Switches

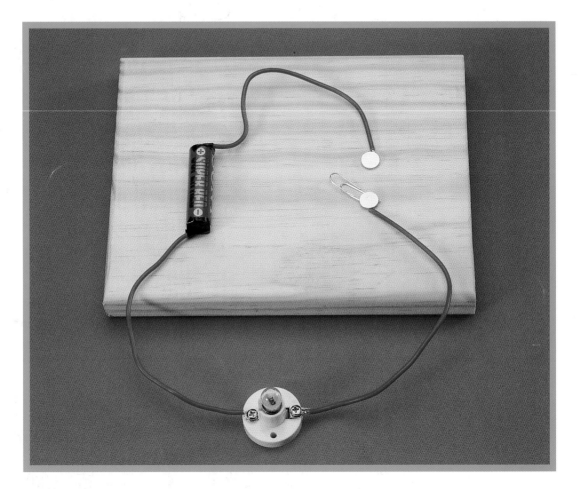

A **switch** is a way of breaking a **circuit**. When the paper clip switch is on, electricity flows around the circuit. When the switch is off, the circuit is broken.

This switch controls an electric train circuit. When the switch is on, the train moves around the track. What happens when the switch is turned off?

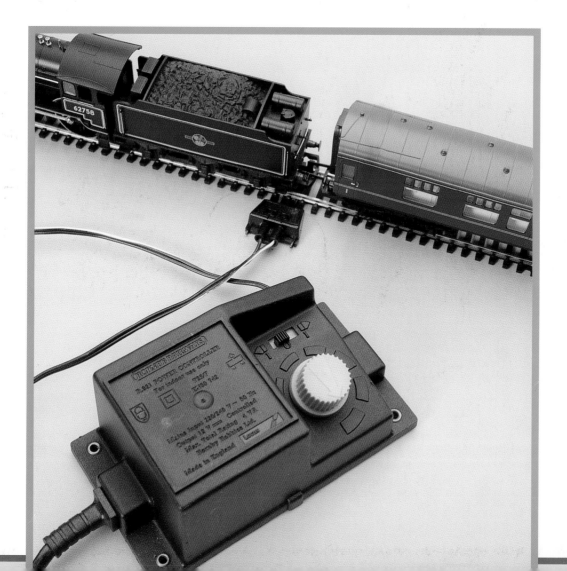

Conductors

A conductor is something that lets electricity flow through it easily. This girl is testing metal foil to see how well it conducts electricity.

Metal foil conducts electricity well.
Metal is a good conductor. It is used
for the wires which carry electricity for
electric trains.

Insulators

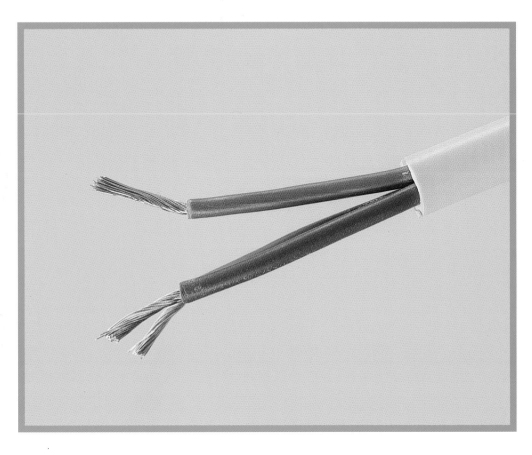

An insulator is something that electricity cannot flow through. Plastic is a good insulator. That is why electrical wires are usually covered with plastic.

This girl is testing things to see whether they are insulators or conductors. When she tests an insulator, the electricity stops flowing.

Drawing a circuit

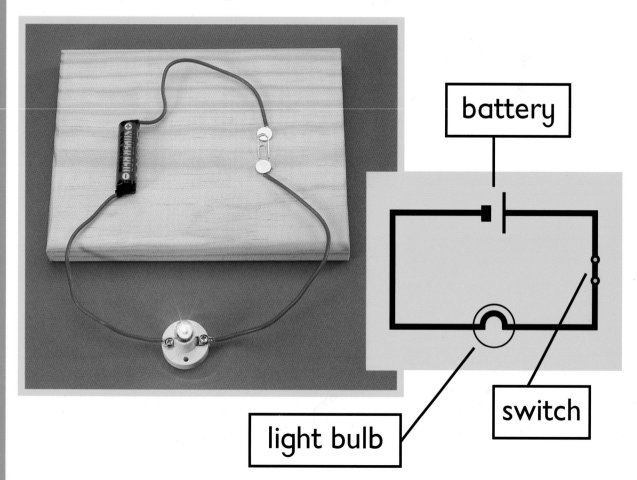

battery

light bulb

switch

You can draw a **circuit** using simple symbols for the battery, **switch**, wire and bulb. Is the switch in this circuit open or closed?

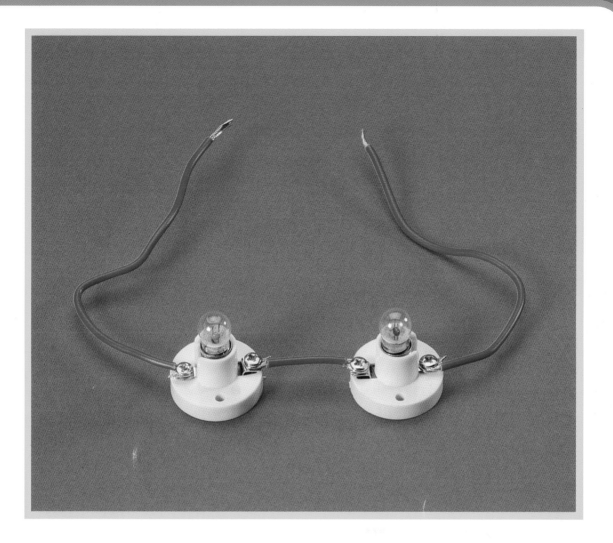

There is something wrong with this circuit – someone has forgotten the battery! Do a drawing to show how the circuit should be.

Glossary

chemical type of substance

circuit pathway for electricity to flow along

force something that makes things move

machine something that uses force to get something done

power strength or energy

power station building where electricity is made

remote control something that allows you to turn a machine off and on from a distance

socket the holes an electric plug is fitted into, usually found on the wall

switch something which opens or closes an electric circuit

Answers

Page 13 – What is a battery?
The remote control needs two batteries to make it work.

Page 23 – Switches
The train will stop moving when the switch is turned off.

Page 28 – Drawing a circuit
The switch in the circuit is closed.

Index

Titles in the *My World of Science* series include:

Hardback   0 431 13700 5

Hardback   0 431 13704 8

Hardback   0 431 13701 3

Hardback   0 431 13702 1

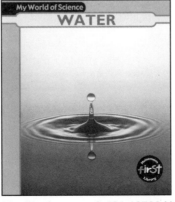

Hardback   0 431 13703 X

Find out about the other titles in this series on our website www.heinemann.co.uk/library